Now I Lay Me Down to Sleep

Action Prayers, Poems, and Songs for Bedtime

Debbie Trafton O'Neal

Illustrated by Nancy Munger

Augsburg
MINNEAPOLIS

May God's loving peace
shelter you
throughout all your days and nights

NOW I LAY ME DOWN TO SLEEP

Copyright © 1994 Augsburg Fortress. All rights reserved. Except for brief quotations in critical articles or reviews, no part of this book may be reproduced without prior written permission from the publisher. Write to: Permissions, Augsburg Fortress, 426 S. Fifth St., Box 1209, Minneapolis, MN 55440.

ISBN 0-8066-2602-X   LCCN 94-71213

The paper used in this publication meets the minimum requirements of American National Standard for Information Sciences—Permanence of Paper for Printed Library Materials, ANSO Z329.48-1984. ∞™

Manufactured in U.S.A.   AF 9-2602

Contents

A Sleepytime Prayer

 Jesus, you have a loving heart.

 Help mine be loving, too.

 Jesus, you have a happy smile.

 Help mine be happy, too.

 And Jesus, you have gentle hands.

 Help mine be gentle, too.

Help me, Jesus, every day,

 in all I do and all I say.

Amen

Now I Lay Me Down to Sleep

Now I lay me down to sleep.
I pray the Lord my soul to keep.
May angels watch me through the night
and wake me with the morning light.

Now I lay me down to sleep.
I pray the Lord my soul to keep.
God's love stay with me through the night
and keep me safe till morning light.

Hush!

Traditional   Traditional

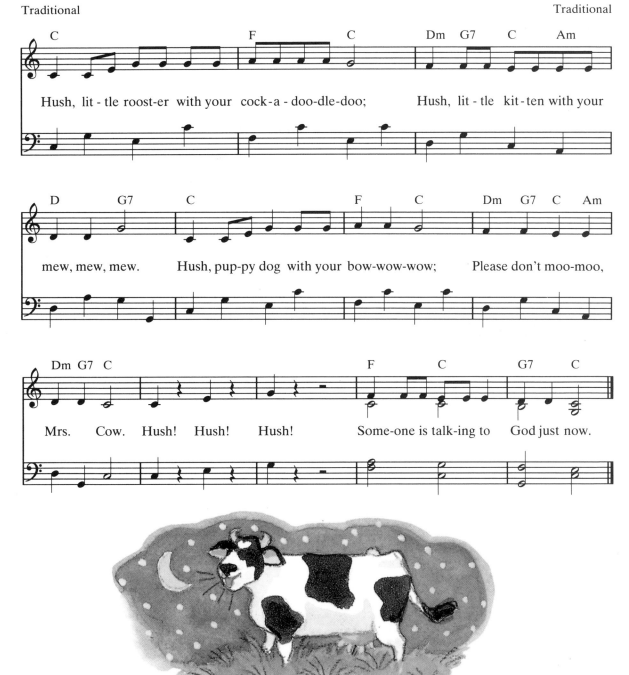

Hush, lit - tle roost-er with your cock-a - doo-dle-doo; Hush, lit - tle kit-ten with your

mew, mew, mew.   Hush, pup-py dog with your bow-wow-wow; Please don't moo-moo,

Mrs.   Cow.   Hush! Hush!   Hush!   Some-one is talk-ing to   God just now.

I Am a Child of God

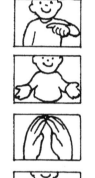 I am a child of God

and God has sent me here.

God's given me a loving home

with family, kind and dear.

8

I See the Moon

 I see the moon.

 And the moon sees me.

 God bless the moon.

And God bless me.

9

Dear God, I Thank You

Dear God, I thank you every time I pray:
for keeping me safe through the day,
for blessing me with your love and care,
for teaching me to give and share.
Bless my friends and bless me, too,
in everything I say and do.
Amen

All Through the Night

Old Welsh Air

1. Sleep, my child, and peace at-tend thee, All through the night;
2. While the moon her watch is keep-ing, All through the night;

Guard-ian an - gels God will send thee, All through the night;
While the wea - ry world is sleep-ing, All through the night;

Soft the drow-sy hours are creep-ing, Hill and vale in slum - ber sleep-ing,
O'er thy spir - it gen - tly steal-ing, Vi - sions of de - light re - veal-ing,

I my lov - ing vig - il keep-ing, All through the night.
Breathes a pure and ho - ly feel - ing, All through the night.

God Made the Sun

 God made the sun,

 and God made the trees.

 God made the flowers,

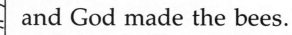 and God made the bees.

 Thank you, God, for the sun

 and the trees.

 For colorful flowers

 and buzzing bees.

For the sounds I hear

 and the sights I see.

 But most of all,
thank you for me!

13

I Will Not Fear

I will not fear
for God is near.
Through the dark night
as in the light.
And while I sleep
safe watch does keep.
Why should I fear
when God is near?

Jesus, Tender Shepherd

Mary L. Duncan

John Stainer

1. Je - sus, ten - der Shep-herd, hear me; Bless thy lit - tle lamb to - night;
2. Through this day thy hand has led me, And I thank thee for _ thy care;
3. Let my sins be all for - giv - en; Bless the friends I love so well;

Through the dark - ness be thou near me; Keep me safe till morn-ing light.
Thou hast warmed me, clothed and fed me; Lis - ten to my eve - ning prayer.
Take me, Lord, at last to heav - en, Hap - py there with thee to dwell.

Open, Shut Them

Open, shut them.
Open, shut them.

Give a little clap.

Open, shut them.
Open, shut them.

Lay them in your lap.

Creep them, creep them,
creep them, creep them,
right up to your chin.

Open up your smiling mouth,

but do not let them in.

Open, shut them.
Open, shut them.

To your shoulders fly.

 Then like little bluebirds,
let them flutter in the sky.

 Falling, falling, falling, falling
almost to the ground.

 Quickly pick them up again
and turn them round and round.

 Faster, faster,

 slower, slower.

 Give a little clap.

 Open, shut them.
Open, shut them.

 Lay them in your lap.

Thank You, Dear Lord, for Evening Rest

Thank you, dear Lord,
for evening rest
after my busy day.
Thank you for guiding me each hour
in all I do and say.
Most of all, thank you for love
from family and from friends.
Help me to share your love with them
when a new day begins.
Amen

Dear Father in Heaven

J.R. Weber
Harm. Robert Wetzler

Anonymous

Dear Fa - ther in heav - en, Look down from a - bove;

Bless fa - ther and moth - er And all whom I love;

Bless fa - ther and moth - er And all whom I love.

A Ladybug

 A ladybug crawls up your arm

 and sits right on your nose!

 A ladybug slides down your arm

 and hops onto your toes!

 A ladybug creeps up your leg

 and lands upon your knee.

 Then scurries to your folded hands

and snuggles down to sleep.

My Five Senses

Thank you, God, thank you
for everything I hear and see:
for chirping birds and buzzing bees,
for sun that brings the morning light,
and moon and stars that shine at night.
Thank you, God, thank you!

Thank you, God, thank you
for everything I touch and smell:
for flowers on my window sill,
the silky fur on my kitten's head
and pillows on my cozy bed.
Thank you, God, thank you!

Thank you, God, thank you
for everything I taste that's good:
for water cold, for favorite food
for vegetables and fruit I eat,
for bread and milk and cheese and meat.
Thank you, God, thank you!

Doxology

Thomas Ken, 1637–1711

Louis Bourgeois, *cir.* 1510–1561
Genevan Psalter, 1551

Praise God, from whom all bless - ings flow; Praise him, all crea - tures

here be - low; Praise him a - bove, ye heaven - ly host;

Praise Fa - ther, Son, and Ho - ly Ghost. A - men.

This Is the Church

 This is the church,

 and this is the steeple.

 Open the doors

 and see all the people!

 Close the doors
and the people all pray.

 Open the doors
and they all walk away.

25

Now the Busy Day Is Done

Now the busy day is done.
Jesus, bless us every one.
Keep us safely through the night
until we see the morning light.

26

Lord, Teach a Little Child to Pray

Ascribed to Jane Taylor

F. Melius Christiansen

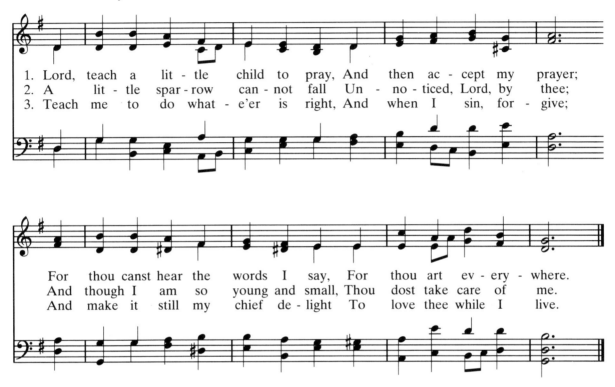

1. Lord, teach a lit - tle child to pray, And then ac - cept my prayer;
2. A lit - tle spar - row can - not fall Un - no - ticed, Lord, by thee;
3. Teach me to do what - e'er is right, And when I sin, for - give;

For thou canst hear the words I say, For thou art ev - ery - where.
And though I am so young and small, Thou dost take care of me.
And make it still my chief de - light To love thee while I live.

Music from *The Primary Hymn Book*, copyright © Augsburg Publishing House.

Two Little Eyes

 Two little eyes to look to God,

 two little ears to hear God's Word,

 two little feet to walk God's ways,

 hands to serve God all my days.

 One little tongue to speak God's truth,

 One little heart for God in youth;

 take them, O Jesus, let them be
always willing, true to thee.

Children of the Heavenly Father

Caroline V. Sandell Berg, 1832–1903
Tr. Ernst W. Olson, 1870–1958

Swedish melody

1. Chil - dren of the heaven-ly Fa - ther Safe - ly in his bos - om gath - er;
2. God his own doth tend and nour - ish, In his ho - ly courts they flour - ish.
3. Nei - ther life nor death shall ev - er From the Lord his chil - dren sev - er;
4. Though he giv - eth or he tak - eth, God his chil - dren ne'er for - sak - eth,

Nest-ling bird nor star in heav - en Such a ref - uge e'er was giv - en.
From all e - vil things he spares them, In his might - y arms he bears them.
Un - to them his grace he show - eth, And their sor - rows all he know - eth.
His the lov - ing pur - pose sole - ly To pre - serve them pure and ho - ly.

Text copyright © Board of Publication, Lutheran Church in America.

Rocka, Rocka

Rocka, rocka,
sleepy child.
Kiss your little head.

Sweetly, sweetly
give a hug.
Tuck you into bed.

Gently, gently
fold your hands.
Bow your head in prayer.

Softly, softly
talk to God.
Thanks for being there.

Taps

Day is done,
gone the sun
from the lakes
from the hills
from the sky.
All is well,
safely rest,
God is nigh.